About the Author

Joanna loves adventure. She loves exploring the world, the verdant corners of Ontario and her backyard. She knows that no matter who you are or where you are, all journeys begin on the inside and that sometimes all it takes is a little guidance. Let Joanna help you discover your inner weekend warrior. She has proven herself on snow-capped mountains, dusty trails and dense woods but it is her love for kayaking on serene waters that she strives to share with you. Joanna likes to live her life a tad left of normal, it is more fun that way. So, you can expect her adventures to be chalk full of outstanding scenery, local knowledge, quirky tips, secret spots and always a smooth but firm workout. Joanna can be seen getting a good dose of the outdoors in rain, shine, sleet or snow but when she does finally stop for a minute she always has her camera ready. Her amazing photos speak for themselves but this book will make it easier for you to get out there and paddle on.

For fabulous headgear check out Joanna's website:
neckieborn4adventure.com

Dedication

This book is dedicated to my Mom and Dad, Margaret and Kirk Wipper. Together, they taught me a deep love of the outdoors. Also, to our children Emily, Laura and James who carry the torch.

Contents

Introduction

This book is the result of a summer of wonderful adventures. Due to the fact we work a lot we normally have one day a week off to play, we had to make the day count.

Every week, I went through a car full of maps planning our one day of serenity. Once I found an area that seemed worth exploring, I would start Googling to make sure we would not end up having a lengthy portage, or worse - kayaks going over a waterfall! Our goal was to be with nature comfortably, learn a little history and visit places we had never been before. A little lunch, ice cream or a dip along the way was the mandate for the day.

Our trips ended up being more than we could ever imagine: the glassy waters, reflections and wildlife gave us so much badly needed peace.

Kayaking is a relatively new sport for us. I grew up being a devoted canoeist. My father, the late Kirk Wipper, was owner/director of Camp Kandalore and I have been canoeing since I could walk.

I have found being in a kayak, skimming across the water feels effortless and works your core. We are middle to older athletes and we have battle wounds from past sports, overworked backs, knees and shoulders. One of the benefits of kayaking is comfortable seats with lots of support. Another benefit - comfortable seats with lots of support. This is a sport you can do, so get out there!

Read on and enjoy the adventures of "Pongoman" and "Pelican Girl". Each trip brought something different to the table. By the way, we never listened to the weatherman who constantly called for rain. We went rain or shine and only experienced one light sprinkle. I remember days where the morning skies were black and by 10.00 or 11.00am, there was brilliant sunshine. So, again, no excuses - just do it!

The trips in this book provide approximately 4-6 hours of enjoyable kayaking.

You will notice I love photos. I've included an abundance to share the unbelievable beauty of these trips with you. Enjoy!

Trip 1
Six Mile Lake Provincial Park near Coldwater, Ontario
May 18

We headed off to Six Mile Lake for our first outing. The local marina afforded us a sandy beach launch - the absolute best take off for bad knees. We were instantly delighted to find the area teeming with wildlife. The trees were wearing their fresh green of Spring. We were met with turtles, trilliums and beaver dams.

On the first leg of our voyage, we came across the rare spotted turtle; boxy looking with a bright yellow throat. I had never come across one before and was fortunate to capture an exceptional photo.

The shoreline revealed one delight after another. The woods along the shoreline were brimming with white trilliums and we had a loon leading the way. Touring the lake we ended up at a sandy beach in the provincial park. We lay on the warm rocks in the sun for a well deserved nap and enjoyed a picnic. It was at this time during a trip to the outhouse that I spotted an American Redstart. At first I did not know what this bird was. It was very small, and fanned its wings like a butterfly or fairy. At last it landed and I was lucky to get a clear shot to share. There were many new vistas, paddling around the lake: bleak rocks, dense woods, lovely lichens, artistic stumps and the biggest perk - no bugs. As a matter of fact we enjoyed a relatively bug-free summer. The only mosquito bite I received was in a restaurant!

Honey Harbour, Georgian Bay
- Little Beausoliel Island
May 19

It was a hot summer day with brilliant sunshine. We launched from a perfect sandy lagoon just on the other side of the village of Honey Harbour. Georgian Bay has a very different landscape compared to our previous adventure: rugged, vast landscapes and pebbled islands. It is more exposed, windier and there is more boat traffic. Choose a calm day for this outing. Georgian Bay can have big water - sudden squalls and big waves. I learned how to surf large boat wakes and this activity became a huge delight of mine. Boaters looked at me strangely when I headed for their massive wake, quickly turning my kayak around and riding a wave to shore. For me this was survival. I have a small kayak and if I did not learn how to catch a wave there was a good chance of being submerged.

My husband with his 140 Pongo, a large, fairly open kayak rode the waves with ease and cut through the water like a breeze. He's at one with his kayak - like an extension of his body which gives him a freedom that his worn out knees no longer allow.

We arrived at a beautiful sandy narrows that was too small for power boats. It offered perfect protection for a picnic and swim. This passage, called Little Dog Channel, divides Little Beausoliel Island and provides a route to the other side of the island away from boat traffic.

When we turned left outside of the channel, we saw a completely different vista: treeless rocky islands stacked with painted turtles. I had never seen so many painted turtles but if I were a painted turtle I would choose to live there also.

Continuing along our way a small Massasauga Rattler swam next to my kayak. I had never viewed one that close before. We came to a rocky cove and I noticed bubbles right next to my kayak. I thought maybe a loon was surfacing. Wrong! A white masked face suddenly peered up at me and I almost dumped in my surprise. A lady yelled from the shore, "Is that a seal? It is huge!" I followed this animal all over the bay trying to get a photo. Unfortunately, it got annoyed and ran ashore. It was at least 5 feet long with sleek black hair and a white mask.

My Dad taught me a great deal about wildlife. He was a real Nature Guru and had a television show called "A Walk with Kirk". The only animal that fit the description of what I saw is the Giant River Otter from the AMAZON. To this day I would love to go back and just wait for this "Loch Ness Monster". That is the way this creature's tail looked - looping like a serpent when it dove. My mysterious friend was the highlight of this trip. We continued along the shore until we reached Big Dog Channel and made a left to return to Honey Harbour and our landing beach. What a day!

Trip 3
Port Severn
May 25

It was a cold, very windy day. We wore our down vests. This location was the perfect choice of destinations for such a day. After breakfast at the local diner, we parked at the free parking lot just up the street on the corner in Port Severn, which is in front of the waterfront park. We launched from the park's sand beach and off we went following the waterway - about the width of a road. It offered much needed protection from the wind. It was a beautiful winding route. The first yellow water lilies of the season were in bloom. There was a Great Blue Heron at every turn. Turtles were in stacks on the logs, snappers and painted enjoying the early sun. My husband and I both agreed we could live here. I named this route "The River People" because much of the twisty waterway had cute cottages that offered everything needed to enjoy an out of doors lifestyle. To my delight, there were a couple of sanctuaries along the river - not to be missed. We wove in and out of this water road enjoying surprises at every turn including a small river otter playing around. We docked for a while to enjoy the sun.

To end our journey, we paddled across the bay to the marina and another sand beach. The marina had a great little restaurant called The Driftwood Café. We enjoyed shrimp and beer - the perfect end to a perfect day!

This trip is for all levels of kayakers. I would choose to make this journey on a cool or windy day probably earlier in the season when the water levels are good.

Trip 4
Moon River

Trip 4
Moon River
June 2 and July 13

Bala is a gem of a town – a must-see. A perfect little village by a waterfall. We stopped at a little café to ask where we could find an easy launch. A helpful man gave us quick directions to a waterfront park complete with beach and free parking. I have always been attracted to the Moon River. I play the tune on my guitar. For years I have driven by the Moon River highway sign on my way north.

It was a chilly, windy day but we ventured on. The water level was very high and most of the docks on the lake were submerged. We stayed close to the shore enjoying the scenery . We turned around a point onto a more open part of the lake and were hit by huge winds.

We had enjoyed a good outing for the kind of day it was so far, but decided if we continued, the waves would win and the water was cold. Turning our kayaks about face, and heading back towards the falls was a wonderful ride. I surfed the entire way back. Kayak surfing is a blast!

After a good work out we were hungry. We had a great hot meal at a little grill called Bee Jays which also offered a view of the river. Bala also has a retro ice cream-cappuccino store and I highly recommend it. My husband and I decided we would return to the Moon River during more favorable conditions and we did.

When we returned on July 13, it was a hot summer day and the water levels had dropped. We began our day having breakfast at a little café overhanging the river, then headed back to the local beach for our launch. We enjoyed a quick swim before take off on this glorious day.

The landscapes changed to visions of the northern shield once we passed through the wide part of the lake to the narrower channels. I have a preference for the narrow passages, because you can visually explore both shores. The scenery gets better with every bend in the river. We landed on some small rock islands bordered on one side by rapids and on the other a calm pool. Here we took a break and enjoyed glorious swim in the quiet cove. We realized this was a better time of year to visit these rapids. They would have been a different animal in the Spring and it was fortuitous we turned back before making it this far in June.

11

We ended our swim with a snack on the small rocky islands, all the time being in awe of this beautiful spot we had come across. Now refreshed, we carried on down the river exploring one lovely scene after another. We headed home after a grand tour, pausing again at our swimming hole for a swim.

Not everything goes as planned - and then it happened! After our swim, I tried to get back into my kayak. I slipped and my kayak paddle snapped in two. Thank goodness for Pongoman. He lassoed my kayak with our safety rope and towed me all the long way back to the landing. I rewarded him with an ice cream in Bala at the great retro ice cream store. Moon River is everything the song says it is.

Trip 5
Port Sandfield, Lake Joseph
June 16

Diversity is the key to enjoyment; new scenery, new experiences. This trip was a tour of lifestyles of the rich and famous. We started our trip on a quaint sandy beach on the far side of Port Sandfield. We were greeted by a group of just hatched ducklings who were very curious about our presence. After starting out from a cove, a very different world appeared. We saw huge boathouses sporting chandeliers and even larger cottages. Then, came very big boats with even bigger wakes. I perfected surfing in their wake which was a saving grace, otherwise I may have been submerged in my small kayak. I suggest everyone to learn to surf a wake - it is great fun. Just don't ride it into the shore.

Back to the cottages: In this area, is a mix of grand old cottages and new opulent vacation mansions. This is where the Muskoka boathouse rules. We did not see canoes or kayaks. We saw float planes and jet skis. Wildlife was scarce – in hiding.

This is a different culture; no quaint cottages with wood fireplaces or woodstoves, where the living is meant more in harmony with nature. Different strokes for different folks. We enjoyed viewing this scene.

We stopped at the docks in Gravenhurst for a well earned dinner on the way home and what should we see? Wildlife on the wharf in town. The most beautiful example of a Lunar moth appeared at sunset. Its antennae feathered to perfection waiting for the moon to appear. This trip is best on a day that is not windy.

Trip 6
Muskoka River to The Falls
June 23

Muskoka Outfitters in Bracebridge makes this trip a breeze. You rent the kayak onsite. Conveniently the Muskoka River borders their property. The Muskoka Outfitters staff will kindly put the kayak in the river for you. They supply you with life preserver, paddle and safety kit. You may choose to journey left to the waterfall or take a longer trip to Lake Muskoka. On this day, with two of my children, we chose left to the falls. Venturing down the river with our daughter Emily and son James racing along, we had an easy and enjoyable trip. The Muskoka River offers classic northern scenery without the boat traffic and very few cottages. Large trees and rock outcrops line the shoreline. A slight currant carried us along like a ride at Disneyland. We followed a passage under a bridge that led to a secret pool. The scenery was very lush - the trees bending over the river offering shade and protection from hot weather. The river ended with a pond and waterfall to complete the picture. This trip would be easy any time of kayak season and a nice introduction for those wishing to try this sport.

This is the shortest kayak trip in this book. It's like a pleasant stroll with solitude and the sound of rushing water. The falls create the perfect backdrop for a picnic or lounge on the rocks and a little swim. We floated for awhile enjoying the view and then turned back down the river, stopping in Bracebridge for a well deserved ice cream cone.

Trip 7
Muskoka River to Lake Muskoka

Trip 7
Muskoka River to Lake Muskoka
June 30

This trip is a 20 km ride for an ice cream cone and totally worth it - the rainbow so to speak. My husband and I made a right turn from the Muskoka Outfitters dock. Under the bridge and away we go.

This is a long route and some areas are more populated than the left turn route in Trip 6. There are sandy shores for picnicking along the way. Ferns, lichens and mosses offer a colourful collage along the banks. A Belted Kingfishers led us along the river dipping and diving all the way. This is a beautiful, easy route.

Now for the excitement! We were paddling along with nature when around the corner blasted a very large boat complete with reindeer, candy canes - and here comes Santa Claus!   It's a narrow river, my kayak is small and the boat's wake was big. I glanced at the tsunami coming towards me and headed for shore. My husband, better known as Pongoman was golden in his 14 foot kayak. My frantic landing was fortuitous as we had landed at the Santa's Village ice cream store. (We needed ice cream for energy of course!) We did not have our wallets so I offered to leave something for ransom in exchange for 2 ice creams, but they were very trusting we would return later.

The Lady Muskoka paddleboat also passed by, slipping around the corner looking like a Showboat out of New Orleans. We carried on past a couple of quaint old Muskoka cottages and finally arrived at a very large opening to Lake Muskoka. We soaked in the view and turned back down the river to Bracebridge.

Trip 8
Mariposa Folk Festival – Cultural Trip
July 5

Last year we went to the Mariposa Folk Festival. It was incredible. Pongoman and I looked at each other and wondered why we had not attended before. So, I decided we must return to the area for a kayak journey.

Our deep interest in history attracted us to the Stephen Leacock Museum. The museum is beautifully situated on a point across from the festival site on Lake Couchiching, near Orillia and makes for a pleasant, leisurely, outing. On the museum grounds there is a wonderful café right on the water with a picturesque view of Stephen Leacock's boathouse. If partaking in the café, I recommend the wild mushroom soup - it is delish.

When Stephen Leacock first purchased this property, the family lived in tents before building a beautiful cottage and grounds. Once you have enjoyed all this site has to offer, there is a small beach where you can launch your kayak for very easy access.

I shadowed the shore, as Lake Couchiching can really kick up some rough water. It is a very shallow lake and sandy. I was always in the position that if I took water in, I could pretty much stand on the bottom and empty out my kayak.

The Mariposa Folk Festival has stages set up all along the shore. I listened to great music on three of the stages from my floating seat - a real treat as you can imagine. I headed home decked out in a new Mariposa T-shirt, thinking "another day well spent".

Trip 9
Oxtongue River and Nature's Jacuzzi
July 21

We started this beautiful day with breakfast in Baysville at a table overlooking Fairy Falls at Miss Nelle's Antique and Café. Breakfast is essential, because with kayaking, you don't always know when you will eat next and you need the protein. This is a great little café with all kinds of homemade goodies and Muskoka coffee. We headed up to the Oxtongue River where Algonquin Outfitters is located just off Highway 60 on the west side of Algonquin Park. There is the perfect access beach across the road from the Outfitters store. You can rent kayaks on sight if needed.

We began our trip going left and circled around a small lake. We carried on past the Algonquin Outfitters beach on our right and headed under the road bridge. We hugged the left shore heading towards the Oxtongue River and Ragged Falls. White water lilies were in full bloom, bobbing up and down with the current. The "carrot" for this trip is definitely Ragged Falls. It is nature's Jacuzzi at its best - whirling, bubbling warm water churning in all directions. We enjoyed a snack in the middle of the falls. The colours were lush and lighting warm. On our return journey in the evening, we passed purple Pickerel weed. A busy muskrat flanked the shore looking for its meal, but the most amazing sight was a very large and statuesque American Bittern. It stood motionless on the shoreline. Its eyes gleamed gold in the glow of the evening sun. To complete our day, we stopped at our favorite pub on Highway 60, called The Cookhouse. The river is well protected, so this trip is great for everyone - a great starter trip for sure.

Trip 10
Coldwater River and the Giant Beaver
July 28

We began our trip up Hwy 400 to Swift Canoe and Kayak. You can rent a kayak and take off right from the site dock. The vistas here are very unique. You commence your journey across open water paddling on a surface layer with giant water lilies. The shoreline is lined with grand reeds that tower over your head. Rock outcrops are covered with bright orange lichen. A pure white snowy egret fishing for its breakfast was standing in the tall reeds. As we got closer, it took to the trees.

The entrance to the narrows is somewhat hidden, but we were able to find the way to the marshland highway. If you come to any forks keep right.

The scenery was completely different from all our other adventures. This was true marshland, the riverbanks covered with wildflowers. Dragonflies were constantly darting in and out of reeds and flowers. This small river winds and twists and looks like the bayous in New Orleans with twisted vines and branches. I half expected to see an alligator.

We passed Arrowhead Orchids shadowing the shore and Purple Fireweed blowing in the breeze. The carrot at the end of this journey is the quaint town of Coldwater. The winding river narrows as you approach town. We were happy and hungry upon arrival, it is a substantial paddle. Turns out, we should have parked our kayaks and scurried up the bank sooner than we did. Instead we got tangled in some fallen trees and shallow rapids - not a good combo. We made it up the river bank just before the old mill and were presented with this delightful town, stopping for pizza, beer and a poke-about. The town is charming, with cafes, boutiques and a Kawartha Dairy – mmm… Moosetracks ice cream! I did a little shopping to support the local economy.

As we headed back to our kayaks, the sun burst forth for our trip home. Earlier, it looked like it would pour all day, and as a matter of fact, by the time we stepped into the car, the sky was black. Even so, we have found it is important to carry on with your plans. We have made adjustments according to the wind and destinations, but our trips have always worked out. All is well that ends well…

In the evening sunlight, the water was like glass and offered a mirror of reflections. As we entered the narrows we heard a huge splash! We saw an animal that looked like a small Hippo. Under closer surveillance we realized it was a beaver - largest beaver I have ever seen. Obviously no predators in this area. I could not believe the size of this beaver so I went home and Googled beavers. They can be a hefty 100 pounds. I was very fortunate to get a photo of the beaver slapping its tail. They move fast, so I was pleased with this shot. As we crossed the final opening back to Swift Outfitters, we spotted a pair of snowy Egrets - one poised motionless on a rock island, the other in-flight, its reflection on the lake. A great finale for the day.

Trip 11

Port Stanton, Sparrow Lake, Trent Severn Waterways and the Swing Bridge

June 16

This trip began at Port Stanton, a historical resort on Sparrow Lake. The homestead of Mr. Stanton still remains today. There is a beautiful little village church that looks like it belongs in a Beatrice Potter book. Also a general store and a breakfast café that serves Kawartha Dairy ice cream.

Good news – there is a sandy beach take off. There are quaint cabins along the shore, and I would love to stay in one someday. We headed across Sparrow Lake towards the opening of the Trent Severn Waterway. With a brisk wind, the crossing was a good cardio workout! We paused at a sandbar across the lake. I had forgotten my drain plug was open and I was now sitting in water.

We glided down the river until we reached the old swing bridge. A boat wanting to pass through blasts its horn and the Bridgeman swings the bridge. It is great to watch this old piece of technology in action. The Bridgeman told us it swung up to 120 times a day. The bridge, which looks like a huge Meccano building set, moves like poetry.

We then continued down the river enjoying constantly changing scenery. Our goal: to go as far as the locks and see them in action. Reaching the locks, we backed off a little as the water rushing out was growing in volume and looked a little threatening. The engineering was amazing and we wished we could pass through but apparently it is a very rough ride. The locks were a fair distance from where our day had begun, so we decided it was time to turn back.

The steamship Lord Stanton built to carry 200 tourists to his resort would have followed the same route we took. It was great to follow the same path of the old Steamships of yesterday. After landing back on the beach on Sparrow Lake, I ended the day with a refreshing swim.

Trip 11
Port Stanton, Sparrow Lake, Trent Severn Waterways

Trip 12
Shadow River, Town of Rosseau

Trip 12
Shadow River, Town of Rosseau
August 22

I discovered this spot online. What caught my eye was the fact that it's a popular river for poets and photographers. It grabbed at my romantic side. I also love discovering all these beautiful little towns with their history and charm. The Town of Rosseau, located at the top of the same named lake was home to the first grand old resort in Canada. This was the beginning of the resort industry. Unfortunately like the fate of many other historical resorts it burned down in 1883. There is a photo plaque in the town showing it grandeur all clothed in white painted wood with great wrap around porches. The town boasts one of the absolutely unmatchable General stores built in 1874. You can find all kind of delectable ginger beer, smoked Gouda, gourmet chips. There is also a great antique and collectibles store. More good news a sandy beach to launch from. The day was hot so I decided to take a quick dip at the delightful beach before kayak take off. The Shadow River is aptly named for the whole river is shadowed by trees and rocks. The river is deep and very narrow. It is a complete Zen experience, smooth water, quiet and no boat traffic. You can truly be at one with nature. There was a little excitement for moi on this journey. Well into our voyage loomed a beaver dam. I thought no problem I have crossed beaver dams before. I hopped out of my kayak and to my great surprise my right leg sunk up to my thigh in heavy beaver mud. I sunk very quickly. Luckily my left leg was firmly planted on some branches. Slightly panicked due to the quickness of the mud I hauled myself out and jumped into my kayak. I was covered in smelly mud. I am sure my husband had a good laugh because his back was turned and he was shaking. Pongoman was smarter. He grabbed a branch from a tree like Gandalf and polled his way over the dam using brute force never departing from his kayak. We carried on further the Shadow River was beginning to diminish until we came to another beaver dam. We turned around. It is my feeling that that this trip would be best in the spring when the water level is at its highest. At the end of the trip we had a swim and nap on the beach. As the sun started to set we headed for home. Just down the road from the town of Rosseau was a gas station that offers great home cooked meals and a very full glass of wine. A perfect end to another day.

Trip 13
Point au Baril and the Shimmering Sands
Aug. 25

As previously mentioned, while out and about, I look for signs and clues for the next trip and that is exactly how this journey took place. I asked a friend if he knew anything about Pointe Au Baril while we were at a coffee shop. My friend said no, but then started pointing to his friend Rob who appeared to walk in on cue. Now Rob just happened to own a cottage on a lovely island at Pointe au Baril. This kind, generous man offered to pick us up in his boat and give us a ride to Hemlock Channel. On route we got stuck in a traffic jam on Highway 11 due to a truck rollover and considered cancelling our plans for the day, but Rob insisted we carry on, and thank goodness we did. Pointe au Baril received its name when some fisherman lost a whiskey barrel in Georgian Bay. The next spring some French speaking fisherman found the whiskey and stuck the empty barrel on the point. Later, a light was placed on the barrel and eventually a beautiful lighthouse was built. Today you can still see the barrel poised on the point for all to view.

Samuel Du Champlain travelled through that very spot in 1612. From further research of Pointe of Barrel on Google, I downloaded many hand painted vintage postcards, which is how I found out about Hemlock Channel, Hole in the Wall and The Grand Ojibway Club.

As luck would have it, our desired destinations were all lined up perfectly, like a constellation. Rob dropped us off at the very end of Hemlock Channel - the perfect starting point. Bleak rocks, clear blue water, sky and brilliant foliage made a stunning backdrop for our paddle. The narrow channels and numerous islands lead to a safe, protected passage in Georgian Bay. I have never seen such an abundance of Cardinal Weed. At the end of the channel we entered the Hole in the Wall, a narrow passage lined with sand. This however, is no ordinary sand; it is The Shimmering Sands. The sand is flecked with mica and shimmers like gold in the water. You feel like you are swimming in a magical place. I felt like a mermaid in a snow globe. Plan this trip for a sunny day so you too will have this experience.

I could see it was everything I had imagined and more. You could go back in time to the grandeur of the day. Wonderful old photos adorn the walls, of steamships and ladies in white linen dresses. We lunched high up on the grand porch feeling like the Kennedy family at Hyannisport. Every detail was as it should be for an old Georgian Bay resort. Lunch was delish and very casual. We strolled around the property and found a kayak landing beach on the back side of the island. Remember this kayak landing beach. We did not know that little piece of info when we set out.

When we arrived at the Ojibwa, my husband looked at the landing dock in front of the resort. It was about 2 feet above our kayaks. That was a problem, as it meant a chin-up onto the dock. My husband was able to hoist himself on to the dock. I on the other hand, have a bad shoulder from a ski race crash, I unceremoniously crawled out of my kayak up the rocky shoreline. I am sure my husband was having a good guffaw behind my back! However, this truly perfect day was worth every scratch and bruise.

On the way home we stopped at the Moose Lodge Trading Post. We love moccasins. We made another stop at White Squall Kayak Center on Highway159 near Parry Sound - a kayaker's dream spot. We stopped at a charming porch café on the Port of Parry Sound. Looking out at the ships sipping a mint julip, we relived this day that was truly a dream!

Trip 14
Nine Mile Lake

Trip 14
Nine Mile Lake

September 1

We had planned a different trip for this day which involved going to a ship wreck in Georgian Bay. All week I checked the weather. It was supposed to be a perfect sunny day with 5 knots of wind. Surprise - it was not to be. Instead, it was a pleasant day, but with lots of wind.

You do not want to be on Georgian Bay in wind. We always have a back up plan and today my husband pointed to the map and said, "What about Nine Mile Lake?" It just so happened Nine Mile Lake was only 4 kilometers away from where we had stopped in Parry Sound to have breakfast.

We started our trip at a beautiful sandy beach and a small waterfront park. To get to this location, take James Street out of Parry Sound, go under the highway overpass and you are there. The day had started with grey skies which quickly transformed into blue skies. Nine Mile Lake is perfect for a windy day. Being narrow and protected, you cannot get into trouble - another great spot for a newcomer to kayaking.

Nine Mile Lake is a sandy lake with steep rocky cliffs. With the change in the weather I took a quick dip, then started our paddling. The rock formations look like Giants, each with its own character, veins of quartz and swirls of granite. Elephant ear lichen clung to the rocks and as I went closer to take a photo, to my absolute delight I spotted a blue tail skink. Unfortunately my camera shutter speed is slow and the blue tailed skink is fast, so I ended up with a photo of the tail only. But at least I have a photo of that wonderful iridescent blue tail.

Onward we went, enjoying one magnificent vista after another, never tiring of the scenery. We stopped for another swim before heading back to the landing. There are very few cottages and we saw only one motor boat. It was relaxing and serene. We had another swim back at the beach landing, and later stopped in Parry Sound for a another harbour side dinner and mint julip. Again a perfect day on the water!

Trip 15
Canoe Lake, Whiskey Jack Bay, Potter Creek
September15

In my opinion, to be truly Canadian, one needs to take this journey. Canoe Lake - Tom Thomson - and the colours all ablaze. Well, 2 out of 3 isn't bad.

It was a beautiful day but without much colour - everything was green. You can see Tom Thomson's memorial totem towering above the trees and it is worth a visit.

We began this day leaving from the Canoe Lake Beach #5 marker on the Algonquin Park map. This offers a very easy access. To get to Canoe Lake, take Highway 60 east from Huntsville. It's a left hand turn a few kilometers into the park and is very well marked.

The morning was crisp with very blue skies. The park ranger mentioned Whiskey Jack Bay and Potter Creek were favourite hangouts of moose, so away we went. We passed sculptural driftwood, and the shore was lined with mighty white pines clinging to the rocks. You can certainly see why this was a favorite haunt of the group of seven. We did not see a moose, as it was a little early in the day. However, a pair of Osprey circled above. Don had a humongous snapping turtle surface next to his kayak. It looked like a tortoise with 100 year old armour. Did you know snappers can be over 5 feet long?

There is no boat traffic in Whiskey Bay. It is all too shallow and therefore perfect for viewing wildlife. We travelled as far up the creek as we could until it became too winding and narrow.

For the next leg of our journey, we stuck close to the left shore. You see more wildlife close to shore and there is usually a band of calm water. We came to the opening of Potter Creek and headed down the river. The remains of a bygone era still stood in the middle of the creek. It turns out this relic-like object was once a bridge leading to a sawmill, now just a silhouette against the landscape. The passage up Potter Creek was peaceful, with undisturbed, calm water and the sun reflected warm light which lit up the landscape. This is the best part of the day to view wildlife.

We startled a beaver and it swam just below the surface right next to our kayaks. I never realized a beaver swims like a porpoise and does not use its legs. At the end of Potter Creek there is a pool and a small waterfall - a great place for a snack or picnic. It's funny how the way back always presents such a different point of view. My eyes were peeled for moose which I had been fortunate to see during the past two trips to Algonquin Park.

We left Potter Creek and headed out across Canoe Lake. Now it was nearing dusk and the wind had picked up. We got a cardio workout and an appetite. We landed at the beach with the sun's rays still upon us. Our reward - the Cookhouse on Highway 60. Yum!

Trip 16
Bon Echo, Lake Mazinaw
September 22

For a grand finale, we wanted to do something spectacular. The season was coming to an end, the winds picking up, the water colder and the days shorter. Nature is aflame with colour at this time of year.

The ancient pictographs on the rocks of Lake Mazinaw were our destination and this trip was to become a spiritual journey. First Nations Shamans travelled into the great granite rocks, fasted and then drew their visions on rocks. This is called a vision quest.

Bon Echo has a great deal of history. In the early 1900's, the Bon Echo Inn was a grand resort. "Back in the day" you could go there to paint and write poetry. The resort's interior was wallpapered with birch bark. This lodge was frequented by members of The Group of Seven. The great rock was a favorite subject of several painters and a Walt Whitman poem is carved into the great rock.

This day trip adventure started on the road at 6:00 am and we were home by 10:00 pm. It was a comfortable trip. We stopped at Mapleton House - famous for maple syrup, and had a wonderful breakfast. Our route took in Highway 11 to Highway 45, then to Highway 169, to Highway 41. This is a beautiful route. It was a true fall day - wind, sun, clouds. An approximately four hour drive flew by because it was so interesting. We passed through several quaint towns. Bon Echo was stunning with huge beautiful trees and sandy beaches. The boat launch is a perfect starting point, as it offers a protected sandy beach on Bon Echo Creek. You may also rent a kayak on site. On this particular day we again rented from Swift Canoe and Kayak on Highway 11. They have the wilderness Pongo that suits my big-man husband so well. We stopped at Bon Echo's Greystone Book Shop and purchased a couple of great books on the history of the area. We toured the remaining part of the Dollywood resort, a clapboard building perched on the hill overlooking the lake. It is chock-full of natural history and the park's history. From this vantage point you may view Walt Whitman's poem through a telescope although we chose to kayak to it. We launched our kayaks from the boat launch on the creek and passed under the bridge to South Lake Mazinaw. I always stick close to the shoreline, as you see a lot more and it is safer. South Mazinaw Lake joins North Mazinaw by a very small narrows.

We headed to North Mazinaw where the great rock is. This rock face is nicknamed "Canada's Rock of Gilbraltar". It was a pleasant paddle to the narrows, but once through, we were met with wind - lots of it - and waves. The headwall went straight up for 700 feet and the water below is 350 feet deep.

There is legend saying that the mighty Mishiphizhew (an Objibway word meaning Great Lynx and God of Waters), lashes its tail in front of the great rock dumping unfavourable travellers. Now, you do not want to be rejected by the great Lynx so there was a lot of pressure! The tail was really thrashing - I had my ski jacket on and wool socks. I was soaked head to toe. My glasses were covered with water droplets. I asked Don to tell me when he saw a pictograph so I could glance while fighting for my life. I leaned back and bent my knees so I would not nose dive to the bottom of the lake going down a steep wave. The weather forecast had said 4 knots, but it was about 20 and no other boats were out there. This was an amazing trip and as the photos demonstrate, it was all worth it. However, my recommendations are make this journey mid-summer when it is calmer and warmer.

If you have time, you can rent a quaint cabin for the night. There is a wonderful hike along the top of the rock.

I had a special goal on this trip. There is a pictograph of a large canoe with people in it. It is this image my father used for The Canadian Canoe Museum in Peterborough. We found the image and of course it was the image farthest along the wall! The pictographs are at the perfect viewing level from a kayak.

Having had a good view of the pictographs, we did not want to push our luck. As soon as I turned my kayak towards South Mazinaw, I caught a wave and surfed back. My kayak was surging and I was flying along on top of a wave. We followed the shore along the lake remembering our great finds. We headed back up Bon Echo Creek past the boat landing. The creek provided a wonderful, peaceful wind-down. It is very protected and at the end a there is a little waterfall. I would recommend attempting this outing when you feel you are an experienced kayaker. For those who can do it, this trip is a must.

We stopped in Bancroft at a wonderful restaurant on the corner called The South Algonquin Eatery and Pub. A good end to a great day!

Trip 17
Twelve Mile Bay
October 14

We decided the weather was too beautiful not to make another trip. It is Indian summer. We chose Twelve Mile Bay as it is close by and being Thanksgiving weekend we did not wish to get stuck in traffic. It is a quick trip up Highway 400, then a left on Highway 12. Take the second right off 12 and you will find the perfect launching spot.

I almost hit the ditch several times trying to photograph the coloured trees through the windshield. We passed a purple hued marsh along Highway 12, full of left over cranberries. From our launch, we first paddled to the right. We wanted to paddle from the very beginning of Twelve Mile Bay to where it joins Georgian Bay. This was definitely the right choice. The scenery at the end of the bay was spectacular. We saw unusual rocks of all colours and shapes covered with a diversity of lichens. I was totally immersed in fall's fabulous colours. Someone asked me if the photos from this trip were colour enhanced and they are not.

Twelve Mile Bay is a good choice for this time of year. It is not too wide so you can enjoy both shores. One side is an untouched reserve.

We travelled up on the sunny side, pausing at the marina for lunch - chili or soup. The marina is perfectly located for you to arrive at lunchtime if you're on the water for 9am. If you complete this trip it is 30 kilometers - a good 6 hour paddle. After lunch we hit headwinds and hugged the right shore. There are several little coves to take a recovery break from the wind and resulting workout. Overall, the whole distance was enjoyable.

We were tired by the time we reached the opening to Georgian Bay. We found a wonderful cove with a black mica sandy beach and stopped for a treat break. Our treats include apricots, nuts humus, cheese and sesame honey crackers. These all help with depleted energy levels. In the sands were perfectly preserved wolf and deer tracks. I find they are always unexpected surprises when kayaking. After stopping, we realized how tired we were and it was a long, long way back. It was going to be a perfect fall evening and as we turned our kayaks towards home, the sun hit our backs giving us some warmth.

The best thing was the wind. The force we had paddled against was now at our backs. We SURFED HOME. It was amazing - you hardly had to paddle. Good thing too, as I could hardly lift my arms. The return trip only took one and a half hours and it was most enjoyable looking at the beautiful scenery passing by at sunset.

I was thinking that all the places we had visited were becoming quiet, deserted and soon would be covered in white. It is a sad feeling as the season comes to an end. We have already started discussing possible places to go next year. There is a lot of fun in the planning and the unexpected is always a real treasure. Just try this sport and you will be hooked.

Trip 17
Twelve Mile Bay

Kayak Rental & Purchasing

There are several good places to rent and purchase a kayak. I highly recommend renting a few different kayaks before you purchase. What we thought we wanted in the beginning has greatly altered to what we want now. Rentals I recommend are Wilderness Systems Kayaks - the Wilderness Pongo 14 is great for a larger man, it was my husband's favourite. The Old Town and the Necky are other common brands that will give you great comfort and a sense of what you may want to purchase for a recreational kayak. For my next kayak, I would like it to be short enough to fit in my van, light so I can carry it myself, and have good back support and storage. I also find I can maneuver a shorter kayak more easily. They surf better.

There are numerous places that have kayak rentals. **Swift** has three locations plus a partnership with **Algonquin Outfitters** on the Oxtongue along Highway 60 which I highly recommend. With **Muskoka Outfitters**, you may leave straight off their docks in Bracebridge. Algonquin Outfitters offer several locations: Huntsville, The Oxtongue, and 2 in the park; access location 11 Lake Opeonogo and access 27 Cedar Lake. **White Squall** offers a paddle center just north of Parry Sound off Highway 400 and another store in Parry Sound. **Sojourn Outdoors** in South Barrie is another option.

The end of summer closed out much like it began with sunshine, calm water, and the familiar swishing sounds of paddling. Paddling kayaks allowed the two of us to explore, discover and regain interest in the beautiful waterways and landscapes Ontario has to offer. We love kayaking it is so effortless and brings one closer to the water . I was a new man once in my kayak the work stress melted away and the world beckoned, and what a world it was. My one day of well deserved sanity.

This summer's paddling season was an excellent one. We paddled nearly every weekend trying to find the perfect places to experience. We found them too. Places of near magic I suppose, offering an inner peace and quiet from a busy world, opportunities to view a lot of diverse nature, and enjoy some exercise at the same time.

It was surprising to both of us that we were the only kayaker's in many of the waters we enjoyed but my feeling was many more would be out here if they only tried it once. We found something special in kayaking a feeling of being one with the world. It is our hope that others will get out and rent a kayak and give it a try.

Let's go kayaking! It's easy, its exhilarating and you feel the sunshine and inhale in all the beauty you can imagine. This summer proved to myself and my wife that your never too old to sit down and just paddle. The seats are comfortable and it's easy on the knees as you go at your own pace. Signing off for this season and excited about next year.

Pongoman and my Pelican Girl.

11472776R10038

Made in the USA
San Bernardino, CA
20 May 2014